The Evolution of the Pterodactyl

The Evolution of the Pterodactyl

EMBARRASSING CONFESSIONS OF A GUY WHO, IRONICALLY, CALLS HIMSELF A SIX-DAY CREATIONIST

ERIC LUDY

Scripture taken from the King James Version®. Public Domain.

ISBN 9781943592098 (paperback)
ISBN 9781943592197 (ebook)

ELLERSLIE PRESS
655 Southwood Lane
Windsor, CO 80550
Ellerslie.com

Published in the United States of America.
First Edition, 2015
Second Edition, 2016

EricLudy.com

CONTENTS

MY FIRST CONFESSION

I might as well kick this book off with my first confession—you know, sort of get it out of the way since I have twenty of them packaged inside this book.

I'm embarrassed to confess this, but this book has absolutely nothing to do with the debate over evolution and creationism. I'm guessing that my title wooed quite a few of the more quasi-intellectual[1] sort that wouldn't otherwise have ever considered reading an "Eric Ludy" book. You see, I've been trying to boost my readership in and amongst that demographic for quite some time. So, I admit it. I saw the opportunity and took it.

But, though it might seem like I'm guilty of a bit of false marketing, this book's title really is spot on. In fact, it's perfect. Because this book has everything to do with "the evolution of the pterodactyl," it is chock full of embarrassing confessions, and I actually am a six-day creationist.

For the quasi-intellectual types, my confession of being a "six-day creationist" might give you the clue that this book probably isn't for you. However, the fact that you actually read four paragraphs of an "Eric Ludy" book is a new record in the Ludy world and a victory I'm sure

1 Oh, by the way, "quasi" means they are apparently or purportedly intellectual but, in actuality, all their impressive high-minded talk and God-defying notions are nothing more than a smokescreen to cover their great ignorance.

I will bask in for the next few years.

This book is classic Ludy. It's unabashedly Christian and strongly biased in the direction of anything and everything biblical, which is the reason many of the quasi-intellectuals look elsewhere for their reading pleasure than the *Eric Ludy Bookshelf of Profundity.* Those that read my books must be able to endure a writing style that is decidedly absent of highbrow vocabulary, liberal slant, and politically-correct conclusions.

I'm a guy who loves Jesus Christ. And, let's face it: loving Jesus and sounding smart just don't mix well.

So, thank you, dear faithful readership who continue to read my books even though they are so socially uncouth. (Or should I just say, "Thanks, Mom!")?

I know I declared that this book was not about the debate between evolution and creationism, but I must forewarn you that I may, every now and again throughout this manuscript, serve up a few juicy morsels on the subject.

For instance, here's a quick thought about evolution:

Evolution is one of those things that quasi-intellectuals believe. They hold passionately to it even though it rests upon a completely unstable foundation of both science and reason. In fact, it takes great faith to believe that everything was created out of nothing. At least the six-day creationist believes that everything was created by a Someone. Both views demand faith. And only one is correct. I'd love to tell you which one is the correct conclusion, but that would possibly make this book about evolution and creationism, which I've already declared it is certainly not. So I will restrain myself.

So, back to the book.

I know this may come as a shocker, seeing as how I'm a six-day creationist, but when I was seventeen years old, I witnessed the evolutionary process firsthand.

And that is what this book is about.

This is a true story about a young guy named Eric Ludy. And though it makes Eric Ludy look absolutely ridiculous, I pray it makes our Great Redemptive God look absolutely amazing.

For out of the "primordial slime" He has saved me. He has washed my leathery skin away.

And I'm happy to declare to the highest heaven and the lowest hell, "The pterodactyl is no more!"

MY SECOND CONFESSION

When I was seventeen, I was stupid.[2]

On the outside, you might have thought of me as a well-behaved kid. After all, I was a nice guy. I got decent grades, used deodorant, didn't smoke, didn't cuss, and went to church on Sundays and Wednesday nights. But, when it came to my home life, I had a serious IQ deficiency.

The year was 1988. It was January. And since it was Colorado, it was also quite cold. But the cold didn't quell my stupidity. I guess when you are stupid, it doesn't matter how cold it is outside; you still keep acting stupid.

The evolutionists believe that life formed out of a "primordial slime". And, they have an interesting point. Because something really does grow out of slime, but it's not life.

My "primordial slime" had three key ingredients bubbling and boiling inside it.

2 I realize that the quasi-intellectuals still reading may argue that this stupidity still lingers in the forty-four year old version of Eric Ludy. I will not debate this point. I was headed down to visit my accountant the other day. I got into the car and started driving. After about ten minutes, I couldn't remember where I was going. I figured I must be headed to the local Starbucks to work on my sermon. I parked. Enjoyed a Venti Iced Chai. Passed a couple hours preparing for my Sunday sermon and then suddenly… oh no! It came to me. A couple hours late, but it came to me. And "stupid" was the only word appropriate to describe what I thought about myself in that moment.

Ingredient #1:
sophomoric[3] arrogance

Ingredient #2:
an uncanny streak of foolishness

Ingredient #3:
an amazing capacity for self-justification

And out of this slime, grew a squawking pterodactyl.

3 Sophomoric comes from two Greek words. 1) *Sophia* meaning wisdom, and 2) *Moronic*, meaning, well . . . ahem . . . moronic. So, I hate to break it to you, all those of you that are currently sophomores, but *sophomore* means "a moron who thinks himself wise."

MY THIRD CONFESSION

When I was seventeen, I also thought I was quite funny. Now that I'm forty-four, I'm fairly confident that my humor is actually only funny to around 7% of society. But back in those days, I was pretty confident that I could get 98% of the vote with any "knock-knock joke" I let fly.

Combine a strange sense of humor with the three dangerous ingredients boiling inside my "primordial slime" and you have the script for quite a story.

It all started that cold January day when I was a comedic seventeen-year-old. I had been working all day long on my image. After all, when a guy is seventeen years old, image is just about everything.

My project that day had been on my "cool persona." The "cool persona" is not something that teenagers ever talk about. Because to talk about it would be totally uncool. Cool is just one of those things that, as a teenager, you just want to exude—making it seem like it just naturally flows from your pores. The goal is to come across like "cool" is just you. You don't want to make it look like you practice "cool" but that you just are "cool." And since I wasn't "cool" inherently, I was doing some behind-the-scenes practicing.

It was during this practicing that I said "it" for the first time. When "it" first came out, I didn't realize how much stir "it" would create. But, that January, a single-celled organism emerged out of the slime—known simply as "it."

I was looking in the mirror when it happened, and with smoldering eyes and a super-cool upward snarl of my top lip, I muttered it:

"Big Tough!"

It wasn't a profound phrase, but it worked extremely well for my purposes. It was clean of all obvious filth, which would mean I could say it anywhere (at church, or even around my mom), and it was still meaty with the necessary teenage angst required to work as an indirect insult.

It functioned like this.

If I was in the mall strutting around and I saw another wanna-be guy acting like he was all that and winking at some girls, it was in that precise moment my tool of "Big Tough!" worked best. To prove my dominance and my disapproval of all male competition, I merely muttered the words, either under my breath, or to the guy strutting through the mall next to me.

"Big Tough!"

If I was a bear or a dog then "Big Tough!" would have been my growl. Girls, it's hard to explain why guys "growl." I guess it's an alpha male sort of thing.

And this alpha male utterance began to catch on. And soon, this single-celled "it" grew two black leathery legs and began to walk.

MY FOURTH CONFESSION

Older brothers have a big responsibility for setting the right example for their younger siblings. And, long and short, I didn't do so well in this regard.

I was a pretty stinky older brother. And as a result, my brother caught the "Big Tough" disease the way a poor, sickly child in the East End of London in the mid-1600s might have caught the Bubonic plague.

Pretty soon we were the "Big Tough" Ludy brothers strutting everywhere with the growl almost constantly on our lips. Every guy around us was a wanna-be, and we Ludy boys were the ones who could discern between true manliness and whatever that "Big Tough" ridiculous was over there near the Taco Bell counter in the Crossroads Mall food court. I mean, come on—is that for real? Sure, the girls all flock to the guy, but look at him, he's... he's... he's (and then we would say in unison)... he's *big tough!*

My younger brother's name is Mark. I called him Marky back then (and still do, though now he is a full-grown guy with beard, wife, kids, and career). He's a really funny guy. And though it has taken me forty-four years to admit it, he's funnier than I am. Where my humor is received with 7% societal approval ratings, his is upward of 13% or maybe even higher. Which for Ludy Humor Standards

(LHS is the official acronym) is quite impressive. I could be jealous of his comedic success, but then I would need to confess that inside this book, too.

Please note: My fourth confession isn't that my brother outshines me in the comedic department, but that I am responsible for injecting "primordial slime" into my younger brother's soul back in early 1988.

I'm so sorry, Marky.

MY FIFTH CONFESSION

Let's face it. A young set of brothers, both trying to be funny, with the "Big Tough" disease spreading quickly through their adolescent bodies, is the set up for one very clear and obvious situation: a Ludy momma that isn't too happy.

With the last name of "Ludy," we, the proud bearers of that lucid and clear-thinking name, are all just a few letters shy of becoming "Loony." So, my mom, already possessing the "L", the "oo" sound, and the "y" on the end, was already vulnerable. But throw on top of that two aggravating young boys and a loony "n" is knocking on the door begging to come on in and replace the lucid "d."

Ironically, I had a gigantic "N" stitched on the front of my letter jacket when I was seventeen.[4] And that was certainly symbolic to my mom during this season. I confess that I was a pesky and noisome "n" that nearly caused my mother to trade out her sanity for Cloud Koo-Koo Land.

My mom was beside herself with frustration in this time period of my life. She was an English teacher—one of those "Eric, it's 'whom' not 'who'" sorts, that was always refining my grammar of speech *and* my grammar of

4 N stood for Niwot, my high school.

behavior. And, I think for the most part, feeling like she was failing in both.

My vast vocabulary that I had possessed at the age of eleven had dwindled down to about twenty-two words when I reached my seventeenth birthday. This collection of twenty-two words included such helpful words such as "No," "Nothin'" (a useful word if ever an adult asked me what I did that day), "Uh-huh," and various other mutterings which were actually once complete words but now no longer intelligible to that class of people that were not privileged enough to still be in high school. There is nothing quite like the public schools to kill brain cells and destroy the linguistic prowess of a seventeen-year-old kid.

Oh, and there were two other words included in my collection of twenty-two that you are already familiar with: "Big" and "Tough." And these puppies were utilized more than any in the entire collection.

"Big Tough!" I would say as I witnessed a teenage strutter at church.

"Big Tough!" Marky would mutter as he saw another "cool" wanna-be in the mall near the Haagan Daz ice cream counter.

"Big Tough!" I would sneer as I pondered all the swaggerers currently on planet earth. "Big Tough!" Marky would join in.

"Big Tough!" was declared at least 831 times every day in either muttered, mumbled, or mused forms by the Ludy brothers in the stretch of time between February and May of 1988.

But, as all evolutionists understand, for the progression of evolution to take place there is a need for something "spontaneous" to occur—something remarkable. How do two black leathery legs become something more? Well, in the Ludy household something "spontaneous" did occur, something remarkable happened. And it occurred at approximately 3:43pm on May 23rd, 1988—21 seconds into the 43rd minute of the 3rd hour in the afternoon of the 23rd of May in the one thousandth nine hundred eighty-eighth year Anno Domini. At this precise moment, my mom screamed.[5]

And that single scream proved to have within it the power to alter the genetic code of this two-footed walking "it". And out of the primordial stew, the "it" took another step forward in its improbable development. What appeared to be a black slimy wing-like appendage suddenly and inexplicably appeared.

5 I completely made up this date and time. I'm not making up "the scream."

MY SIXTH CONFESSION

At the age of seventeen I was apparently deaf.

Wait a minute. That really wasn't a very good confession. Let me try that again.

At the age of seventeen I didn't listen to my mother.

After "the scream" incident on May 23rd, 1988, a new rule was instituted in the Ludy home.

It was simply known as the "Big Tough Tax." My mom voted the law into effect that fateful day in May and enforcement of this new law went into effect immediately.

Here's how it worked...

If either Marky or I ever said the words "Big" and "Tough" together we were immediately taxed twenty-five cents. And, yes, as painful as it is to admit, twenty-five cents was a big deal back then.

After losing my entire savings of $15.75 in a single day due to the Big Tough Tax, I realized that this was a big deal and a very real threat to my financial future.[6]

This is when Marky and I met in secret for the now famous Synod of Dordt. No, that wasn't the name. What was it? Oh yeah. Ours was called the Synod of Dorks.

We decided that this "Big Tough" thing wasn't working well for us. We both loved saying "Big" and "Tough" together, but the "BT Tax" was killing us both. And it was

6 All documentation of the actual amount lost in that single day has been lost to history. But, suffice it to say, it was enough to make me desperate.

during this famed Synod, held in the cramped loft space above Marky's bed, that we decided on a new cool phrase.

After all, the law stipulated that we would be charged twenty-five cents if we said the words "Big" and "Tough" together. It said nothing about us changing out the words "Big" and "Tough" for two different words.

MY SEVENTH CONFESSION

When I was seventeen, I was worse than Johnny Cochrane (O.J.'s lawyer) when it came to finding loopholes in the Ludy legal code.

It was during the Synod of Dorks that Marky and I secretly swapped out "Big" and "Tough" for "How" and "Dumb."

The new phrase "How Dumb" was an amazing elixir to our taxation dilemma. And it worked. It gave us both the satisfaction of a really juicy insult phrase and was, at the same time, technically not deemed profanity.

"How Dumb" was a brilliant stride forward in the evolutionary development of the "it."

So, for the next three months, we utilized "How Dumb" as our go-to cool phrase of choice. And, truth be told, Marky and I began to prefer it over the previously bulky phrase of "Big Tough." For we noticed that there were certain qualities to the word "How" that we never were able to enjoy with the word "Big." The word "How" could be drawn out in unique ways that allowed different emphases and varying shades of meaning.

But, though this evolutionary leap was truly a magnificent development, it too was short-lived. For mothers can only be fooled for so long.

MY EIGHTH CONFESSION

When I was seventeen I was inordinately stiff-necked. Like the Israelites wandering in the wilderness I was not quick to learn my lessons and certainly not quick to change when corrected.

The "How Dumb Tax" was instituted somewhere in the latter summer months of 1988. My mom signed a law into effect, officially declaring that the words "How" and "Dumb" combined together would immediately result in a hefty tax of fifty cents.

Whoa!

Though it can't be proven in a court of law, there was certainly a public outcry that included the words "How" and "Dumb" combined in a sentence, but it has remained untaxed to this day due to the fact that it was muttered under my breath.

But this time Marky and I were a bit quicker to resolve the problem. After going in the red $3.50 in the first fifteen minutes after the institution of the "HD Law," I got wise.

Important Note: The word "How" had actually morphed by this time into more of a "Ha" (like ha—from happy). So, it was technically, "Ha" plus "Dumb" that equaled a fifty cent tax.

Back to the story...

I remember walking through the Ludy house that warmish day in late August of 1988 and whipping out a loud "Haaa."

My mom peered around the corner, excited to think that yet another fifty cents was soon to be hers. I had already paid plenty in the last twenty-four hours due to this new tax. So there was a heightened sense of need for an evolutionary breakthrough. And sure enough. It was in this moment that the "spontaneous" and the "remarkable" thing happened to cause the "it" to progress in its uncanny development.

The Ludy dining room was in view, and on the wall of the dining room was a picture that my sister had painted, named "Hannah." It was a picture of a Romanian gypsy that my mother cherished.

So, as the "Haaaaa" hung in the air, and my mom waited with bated breath for the conclusive, "Dumb," a sudden alteration of the DNA strand took place, when I finished with "Nuh."

My mom looked at me, confused.

I simply said with a smile, "Hannah. Great picture."

My mom's fifty cent dream had been foiled, and I had suddenly found myself the ultimate legal loophole.

The new phrase of choice for the Ludy brothers immediately became "Haaa Nuh" that day.

And suddenly another black appendage grew out of the side of the black slimy creature. And a flapping sound could be discerned if one listened closely.

MY NINTH CONFESSION

Sin thrives in and through the work of microevolution.[7] It adapts to its environment. Like a peppered moth, it finds a way to hide itself amongst the tree bark of everyday life.

Yes, I'm a six-day creationist. But I am very familiar with the reality of how sinful evolution works. And without a new creation in and through the Cross-work of Jesus Christ, the slime from that primordial stew will continue to produce creatures of black leathery skin, creating a flap in our caveman-like souls.

When I was seventeen, I hid my sin. I was like Darwin's moth, peppering myself with a little "Haaa" and "Nuh" to try and cloak my deeper problem with rebellion and disrespect.

A couple months of "Haaa" and "Nuh" went by before my mother instituted a piggy bank shattering tax of seventy-five cents for every violation. The "HN Tax" was unprecedented. It was enough to send Marky and me into financial ruin. But, the Ludy moths—I mean, the Ludy boys had become experts by this time at microevolutionary leaps.[8]

---

7 Some may question whether or not I am referring to micro or macro evolution here. However, since the quasi-intellectuals don't seem to distinguish any more between the two, but treat them both as the same, I don't see any reason why it would matter if I were to swap one out for the other here. Unless, maybe, there really is a difference between the two?

8 I realize that most quasi-intellectuals have attempted to debunk the

What we had discovered in our use of the "Haaa" was that in and of itself, it could accomplish everything needed for satisfying the insult need while still being hilarious. The "Haaa" had limitless possibilities. And so, the leathery black two-legged, two-winged "it" grew a head and two bulbous yellowish eyeballs.

---

creationist's use of the term "microevolution," but I personally see it as a very useful, accurate, and expressive term. With my tongue-in-cheek, may I remind you that it was these same folks who removed "Pluto" from our list of planets, eliminated the "Brontosaurus" from history, and have downgraded the fifteen foot tall "Irish Elk" to being nothing more than an "Irish Deer." How can these people possibly be trusted?

MY TENTH CONFESSION

When I turned eighteen in December of 1988, I had finally reached the maturity-level requisite to be a full-blown idiot.

It was my senior year in high school. Mr. Boyle's chemistry class was awash with the cacophony of rowdy teenagers and I was sitting next to my friend, Mike. Mike had just done something that earned him a long and emotion-infused "Haaa!"

It was at that moment that I heard "it." It was in Mr. Boyle's classroom that fateful morning in January of 1989 that the black leathern creature grew a beak and squawked for the first time.

I excitedly said, "Mike, hold out your pen!"

"What?" Mike answered, confused.

"Hold out your pen like a perch!" I shouted back.

Mike did it. And the creature's long talons wrapped themselves around Mike's pen and let out a mournful squawk. "Raaaa!"

The five letters "R-a-a-a-a" don't do the sound of it justice. Imagine the sound of a dying "prehistoric" bird mixed with the deep angsty tones of a rebellious senior in high school.

The "it" had now officially been named. It was simply known as "the pterodactyl."

MY ELEVENTH CONFESSION

When I was eighteen I was caught in the downward spiral of sin.

Sin only takes you in one direction... down.

And that was where I was headed. In my attempts to be funny, I had managed to become a idiotic black leather bird.

But, when sin comes to full maturity, it doesn't just sit on a perch and squawk; it flaps its wings and begins to fly. It causes a disruption in the lives of those around you.

And this is precisely what Marky and I began to do. We flew like ugly bats, squawking, landing on people's hairdos, perching on unsuspecting ears. For those of you who are having a difficult time imagining this, just think preschoolers playacting as if they were static electricity. We were loud, rambunctious, and irritating. Of course, we received a lot of laughs. But, my mother was beside herself with dismay.

What does the proverb say... a foolish son is the grief of his mother (Proverbs 10:1).

Hmmm. Yep, that about says it.

In the proceeding year, the evolution of "The Dying Birds" continued unabated. The creature grew more cunning and allusive, more dynamic and loud, more strange and idiotic. And I remember my poor mother sitting across the table from me in this time period and sighing, "What did I do wrong?"

My response was simply to shrug my shoulders and say, "I think you did a great job!" And then I proceeded to take flight and soar around the kitchen squawking.

I'm so, so sorry, Mom!

MY TWELFTH CONFESSION

When I was eighteen I was an idiot. I realize this sounds like a confession I made earlier in the book, but even as I have written these first eleven confessions, I feel that it is necessary to reiterate that central and salient point.

As a forty-four-year-old pastor, I labor every day to see foolishness removed from people's lives. I see the consequences of the "primordial slime" everywhere. I see black leathery creatures, not unlike my own, yapping, clawing, squawking, and slithering all the time and all over the place. Life for me almost feels like a long-term stopover at Jurassic Park.

For most of us, the pterodactyl evolution in our own lives is not so dramatic and loud as it was in my life. For most of us, it's a silent process of doubt, rebellion, disobedience, deceit, and self-justification.

But, it's the evolution of an obnoxious creature no matter how you slice it.

MY THIRTEENTH CONFESSION

I must confess that my motive for writing this little book wasn't to just tell a witty and ridiculous story about my childhood. And, ironically, I didn't write this just to point out to you the cute, comical, thoroughly irritating, yet seemingly harmless pterodactyl flying around my mother's kitchen.

I wrote this in order to point out something far more sinister.

My pterodactyl was, in and of itself, relatively harmless. But there was something deeper, something hidden behind the curtain of my life that was of greater concern.

My pterodactyl didn't evolve on its own. There was something helping it along. Something inspiring me toward disrespect, self-justification, and disobedience. There was a rebellion lurking in the shadows of my soul that was whispering to me, training me for disobedience.

My pterodactyl was somewhat endearing, albeit supremely irritating to some and an outright shame to my mother. But this invisible personality behind the curtain was something altogether different than the pterodactyl. It was entirely grotesque. He was covered with black leather just like my pterodactyl. But he wasn't in any way cute or comical. And he wasn't small. He was huge. As if Godzilla were hiding in the basement of my soul, stoking the fires of sin in my life with his flaming breath.

No one saw this invisible beast. Hence the word "invisible." But what's strange is that even I didn't know he was there. I was being puppeteered, controlled, manipulated, and I didn't even realize it. Unbeknownst to me, this unseen Beast was slowly killing me, conspiring to hide the truth from my sight, whispering to me all day long about the legal loopholes I could take to self-justify and to avoid any form of conviction of sin.

According to the Bible, this unseen Beast is not just lurking in the shadows of my soul, but in every soul.

There are different names in Scripture for this dark power that controls us.

"The Flesh" was the Apostle Paul's term in the New Testament.

But the description that is most in sync with the reptilian theme of this book is found in the Old Testament. In the book of Job, this malevolent creature is described in great detail. And to think that such a beast known as Leviathan would be dwelling in the waters of our soul is terrifying.

After all, he has terrible teeth and is covered with impenetrable scales. He breathes fire and snorts smoke. And his eyes are red like the morning dawn.

Yikes!

MY FOURTEENTH CONFESSION

I was an idiot pterodactyl at the age of eighteen, yes, but I was also, and unbeknownst to me, the loyal servant of "The Fire-Breathing Beast" (heretofore referred to as the Terrible FBB).

If you had asked me back in latter months of 1989 about the Terrible FBB, I would have flatly denied any connection with him. You see, I didn't realize he was controlling me.

According to an eighteen-year-old Eric Ludy, I was merely a young guy with hormones, teenage angst, a large appetite, and a lot of extra energy on my hands. After all, that is what Dr. Phil would have described me as. And isn't he always right?

If I were asked about the evolution of the pterodactyl, I would have explained it as the result of my unique personality and my unusual creative streak.

But, in actuality, there was another mind that was not my own conspiring, teaching, and conforming me into his image. And it was not the sort of image that any one in their right mind would really want to be formed into.

I was a servant of the Terrible FBB and didn't even know it.

MY FIFTEENTH CONFESSION

I thought I was in control of my own life at the age of nineteen. I had graduated from high school and was in college. I had some time to think and consider. God was awakening me, and I was beginning to realize that maybe a lifestyle of disrespect, disobedience, self-justification, and deceit wasn't all that it was cracked up to be.

I decided that maybe I needed a bit more God in my life. Maybe I should show a bit more respect to my mother. Maybe I should be a better example to my brother. And, maybe, it's time to stop flying around the kitchen like a dying bird.

But I found that my New Year's resolutions in the beginning of 1990 proved impossible.

I thought to myself, "How hard can it be to do make these small little moral improvements?"

Yet, it was the strangest thing—I simply couldn't become a better person.

When I tried to show a bit more respect to my mother, I miserably failed.

When I tried to be a better example to my brother, I only seemed to supply him a lesser pattern to follow.

And even when I tried to stop flying around the kitchen like a dying bird, my buddies would beg for the pterodactyl to fly once again, and, sure enough, he got lift-off and started squawking.

What I wanted to do for some reason I couldn't do.

The Apostle Paul talked with me about this problem in the seventh chapter of Romans.

He said, "Eric, I know precisely what you are talking about. When I was a good law-abiding Jew, digging in my own pockets to find the strength to fight off the Terrible FBB, I didn't find the strength to do it either."

In the Bible Paul is quoted as saying,

> *"For what I would want to do, that do I not; but what I hate, that do I... For I know that in me (that is, in my flesh,) dwells no good thing: for to will is present with me; but how to perform that which is good I find not. For the good that I would want to do I do not: but the evil which I would not want to do, that I do... O wretched man that I am! who shall deliver me from the body of this death?" (Romans 7:15,18-19, 24).*

Like the Pharisaical Paul, I was unable to stop sinning. And my sinning was continuing to get worse and worse. Almost as if my yearning to stop sinning only seemed to create more of it.

But, unlike Paul, I hadn't figured out the solution to this problem. Paul had found victory. In his letters to the churches he even seemed to mock the power of the Terrible FBB. He referred to it as defeated, crucified, and dead.

What did Paul have that nineteen-year-old Eric Ludy did not?

For at the age of nineteen, I was suddenly realizing that I was a prisoner. And my prison guard was... uh...one really bad fire-breathing dude.

MY SIXTEENTH CONFESSION

In the spring of 1990, I was one proud nineteen-year-old.

If you ask me how I know that I was proud, it's because I believe the words of Scripture.

When talking of the Terrible FBB (a.k.a. Leviathan), the Bible says that nothing on earth is his equal—he is a creature without fear. He looks down on all that are haughty; he is king over all that are proud.

The Terrible FBB rules the life of all that remain proud.

So, obviously, since I was ruled by the Terrible FBB, then at the age of nineteen I was proud.

And proud I was.

I considered Jesus Christ a wonderful guy. But I honestly thought He was in need of me, rather than the inverse, that I was in desperate need of Him.

I went to church—I just didn't allow all the church stuff to get too close to me. For I believed that church stuff, if taken in too high a dose, makes one rather ridiculous in the eyes of the world.

I wanted to stay in control of my life. But all that Christian stuff was always telling me to lay my life in Christ's hands and trust Him.

This is where the pride came in.

For pride says, "I don't need a Savior." It's only humility that acknowledges need—that cries out in desperation and calls on Jesus to rescue you.

Thankfully, "humility" was right around the corner for nineteen-year-old Eric Ludy. And it couldn't arrive soon enough.

MY SEVENTEENTH CONFESSION

I struggled with hatred when I was twenty.

I'm not the sort of guy that "struggles with hatred." I'm a very easy-going, love-everyone, never-hold-a-grudge sort of guy. So, it sounds quite extreme to admit that I loathed someone when I was twenty.

But it's true. I desperately hated the Terrible FBB.

I realized that the Bible was right. It declared that I couldn't do it myself. And I was ready to admit it.

I wanted to live a life pleasing to God. I wanted Jesus to be glorified in my life. But over and over again I had succumbed to the wicked craftiness of this Terrible Fire-Breathing Beast living in the dormitory of my soul.

I tried everything to root out this Godzilla inside the basement of my life.

I tried intense physical discipline: getting up early for prayer, giving up food, reading Scripture, memorizing Scripture, and attempting with all the gusto in my being to emulate the life of Christ.

But no matter how hard I tried, it seemed to only cause the Terrible FBB to grow stronger. This invisible power seemed to feed off of my self-attempts at righteousness. And the more I disciplined my life, the greater hold this Flesh proved to have over me.

Looking back I see how God leveraged this situation

for His glory.

The holy command came to my soul: "Eric, stop submitting to this Flesh Beast!"

But my soul was powerless to stop him. And my response came back, "But, God, I can't out-muscle him! I don't have the power in me in order to do it."

It was then that I re-read Romans chapter seven. And I realized that the Apostle Paul actually gives the secret to his victory over the Terrible FBB in that very chapter. I don't know how I missed it before. He said, "O wretched man that I am! who shall deliver me from the body of this death?" And then he answered his own question with the triumphant phrase, "I thank God through Jesus Christ our Lord" (Romans 7:24-25).

The command came at me yet again: "Eric, stop submitting to this Flesh Monster!"

And my response came back, "But, God, this Flesh Monster is too strong for me!"

"But, Eric, do you believe that this Flesh Monster is too strong for Me?"

Huh? Now that's a thought!

My life began to transform with the simple logic that Jesus was and is stronger than the Terrible FBB, and that if I trust Jesus with my life, He will do the fighting for me.

And then the thought that revolutionized my life entered my mind.

"Wait a minute!" I pondered excitedly. "He already did do the fighting for me! The battle is already won! The Terrible FBB is already defeated!"

MY EIGHTEENTH CONFESSION

There are two sorts of "confession" in the Bible. One is a confession of sin, while the other is a confession of faith.

I'm happy to say, after seventeen miserable confessions of sin in this book, that this particular one is a confession of faith.

At the age of twenty, my eyes were opened to really see the Cross. I had known about the Cross my whole life, even trusted that the work of that Cross offered me forgiveness from my past mistakes. But I hadn't ever reckoned the Work of that Cross an actual victory, on my behalf, over the malevolent power lurking in the depths of my soul.

Could it be that the Terrible FBB was actually defeated? That he had no power over me? And that he was legally barred from harming me and controlling me anymore?

It was almost too good to be true.

But that is precisely what the Apostle Paul was preaching to my soul. And everywhere I read in the New Testament I was beginning to see it.

And even the Old Testament, in the book of Isaiah, while foreshadowing the mighty victory of the Cross of Christ, declared:

"In that day the LORD with His severe sword, great and strong, will punish Leviathan the fleeing serpent,

Leviathan that twisted serpent; and He will slay the reptile that is in the sea" (Isaiah 27:1).

And this is precisely what I found to be true in my life when I was twenty.

And still, to this day, I have only found it to be more and more true as the years pass.

Jesus is my Victor. His Cross is the great Weapon. His shed blood is efficacious. And the Terrible FBB no longer rules in my body. And the seedbed for the evolution of dumb moves, idiotic maneuvers, boneheaded behaviors, and otherwise self-centered, fleshly acts of ridiculousness is no more.

MY NINETEENTH CONFESSION

I am a new creature in Christ Jesus. My desperate compulsion to do that which is wrong is gone. My yearning to hide my sin is no more. My desire to self-justify my wrong has disappeared. I can now confess my sin as if it is, in fact, wrong. I can agree with God. I can agree with my mom. I can admit my stupidity to Marky. And I can write it all down in a book and share it with you.

These are all supernatural things.

The shed blood of Jesus has changed me. It is no longer "I" (or "it") who lives, but Christ who lives in me. I am no longer a product of the evolution of sin, but a product of a new creation in the shed blood of Jesus Christ.

A delivery truck full of canned primordial soup still stops by my house regularly and offers special deals and many novel incentives to me, in hopes that I will embark upon the evolutionary processes afresh and get back in the bird business. And, yes, the Terrible FBB is still there using his invisible powers to try and sneak back into my life. He baits me with all the world's goods, the world's riches, and the world's pleasures. You know, the standard stuff.

But, I have no interest in such offers.

After all... I have Jesus now.

MY TWENTIETH CONFESSION

By the way. I'm still an idiot.

I'm just no longer an idiot because of my sin. I'm an idiot of a different sort.

The world looks at me as if I'm a buffoon. And that is just what happens when you start telling people to kick the Terrible FBB out of the basement of their souls, when they don't even believe that he is actually living there.

The Gospel of Jesus Christ truly sounds ridiculous to those who are proud and self-justifying in their sin. To those controlled by the Terrible FBB, often such notions as Jesus, Salvation, Rescue, Hope, Love, and Joy—are all just overused empty religious-sounding words. And even a squawking pterodactyl often sounds sweeter to the human soul than the preaching of truth. For pterodactyl squawks are actually sort of funny, while biblical thoughts are like heat-seeking missiles finding that one hidden sin in the soul and stripping it naked before the bright light of heaven.

So, yes, I'm still an idiot.

I guess it would be safe to say that all of us, in a way, are idiots. We just need to make sure we are the right sort of idiot.

Are you an idiot for sin's cause, or an idiot for Christ's sake?

Paul, the great apostle, referred to himself as *idiōtēs*. Which, in the Koine Greek language means exactly what you probably guessed it means: seemingly unlearned, appearing unskilled, and lacking intelligence. And, yes, it is in fact the root of the word "idiot" in the English.

Being a "fool" is easy. In fact, we all come by it naturally. But being the "right sort of fool"—a fool for Christ's sake—is anything but natural.

For that sort of idiocy, we need divine help.

Thank you, Jesus, for setting me free to become a fool for You.

ABOUT THE AUTHOR

There were three things growing up that Eric Ludy declared he would never become: a teacher, a missionary, and a pastor. He became all three. In a vain attempt to gain some credibility he also became a writer. But seventeen books later, he's admitted that this plan backfired big time—the messages contained in his books have led to more scorn than the other three combined. Ludy is the president of Ellerslie Mission Society, the teaching pastor at the Church at Ellerslie, and the lead instructor in the Ellerslie Discipleship Training. He descended from seven generations of pastors, is totally uncool, somewhat skinny, and in Japan supposedly his last name means "nerd." But, that said, he is clothed in the shed blood of His beloved Savior; Leslie, his wife of twenty years, still laughs at his jokes; and his six kids think he is Superman (or at least Clark Kent). So, all is well with the author of this book. He calls Windsor, Colorado home, but longs for his real home in heaven where being a "fool for Christ" finally will be realized to be the most brilliant life-decision any human has ever made.

EricLudy.com

MORE BOOKS FROM ERIC LUDY

Romance, Relationships, & Purity

When God Writes Your Love Story

When Dreams Come True

Meet Mr. Smith

A Perfect Wedding

The First 90 Days of Marriage

Teaching True Love to a Sex-at-13 Generation

It Takes a Gentleman and a Lady

Godly Manhood

God's Gift to Women

Christian Living & Discipleship

When God Writes Your Life Story

The Bravehearted Gospel

Heroism

Prayer

Wrestling Prayer

Memoirs & Confessions

Are These Really My Pants?

Evolution of the Pterodactyl

The Bold Return of the Dunces

Fingerprints of Grace

EricLudy.com

DISCOVER MORE FROM THE AUTHOR

SERMONS

Unashamed Gospel Thunder.

Listen now: Ellerslie.com/sermons

CONFERENCES

Come expectant. Leave transformed.

Learn more: Ellerslie.com/conferences

DISCIPLESHIP TRAINING

A set apart season to become firmly planted in Christ.

Learn more: Ellerslie.com/training

READ MORE FROM ERIC LUDY

EricLudy.com

www.ingramcontent.com/pod-product-compliance
Lightning Source LLC
LaVergne TN
LVHW010108110826
845155LV00028B/542

* 9 7 8 1 9 4 3 5 9 2 0 9 8 *